148

DIAMONDS
Forever

Also by W.P. Kinsella

DIAMONDS Forever

REFLECTIONS
from
the FIELD,
the DUGOUT &
the BLEACHERS

Edited by
W.P. KINSELLA

HarperCollins*PublishersLtd*

For Ken Rivard

The publishers acknowledge the invaluable research and expertise of Russell Field.

Many of the quotations in this volume are well-known and widely quoted.
Acknowledgements begin in the notes, p. 151.

DIAMONDS FOREVER: REFLECTIONS FROM THE FIELD,
THE DUGOUT & THE BLEACHERS
Copyright © 1997 by W.P. Kinsella. All rights reserved. No part of this book
may be used or reproduced in any manner whatsoever without prior written
permission except in the case of brief quotations embodied in reviews. For
information address HarperCollins Publishers Ltd, Suite 2900, Hazelton Lanes,
55 Avenue Road, Toronto, Canada M5R 3L2.

http://www.harpercollins.com/canada

First edition

Canadian Cataloguing in Publication Data

Main entry under title:

Diamonds forever : reflections from the field, the dugout & the bleachers

ISBN 0-00-255758-4

1. Baseball - Quotations, maxims etc.   2. Baseball - Anecdotes.
I. Kinsella, W.P.

GV867.3.D52 1997   796.357   C96-931881-2

97 98 99 ❖ EB 10 9 8 7 6 5 4 3 2 1

Printed and bound in the United States

Introduction

Baseball is conducive to storytelling because of the open-endedness of the game. Other sports are twice enclosed, first by rigid playing boundaries, then by time limits. There is, as we know, no time limit on a baseball game, while on a baseball field the foul lines diverge forever, eventually taking in a good part of the universe. This open-endedness makes for myth and larger-than-life characters, both of which are necessary to good storytelling.

There isn't much in the way of literature involving basketball, football or hockey and I believe it is because these sports offer instant gratification, constant action with players rushing madly from end to end of the playing surfaces. There is no time for thought or reflection. In baseball the ball is in play for around five minutes out of three hours—this makes baseball a game of anticipation, a game for the thinking fan, a game where little gems of wisdom or whimsy can be created in the dugout, the bullpen or the pressbox during long, hot afternoons and evenings of baseball.

A couple of my favorite stories are not included in this collection because of length. One is particularly timely because of the fuss currently being made over Hideo Nomo, the star Japanese pitcher for the Los Angeles Dodgers. This story concerns Masanori Murakami, the first Japanese-born pitcher in the major leagues, who played briefly for the San Francisco Giants in the 1960s. Since Murakami spoke no English, Hall-of-Famers Willie Mays and Willie McCovey volunteered to help him out. The first words they taught him were what he should say when the manager came to visit him on the mound. Murakami was a quick learner. One afternoon when things were not going well, heavy-set San Francisco manager Herman Franks lumbered to the mound. Murakami bowed politely and said, "Get lost, Fatso." That's the story, though I expect the actual phrasing taught to Murakami by Mays and McCovey was considerably more colorful.

Another favorite story concerns the current Seattle Mariners manager, Lou Piniella, when he was a player for the Yankees. Piniella, one of the slowest runners in baseball, was on first when the next batter hit a double. Third-base coach Don (The Gerbil) Zimmer held up his hands to stop Piniella at third. Piniella ignored the sign and lumbered on, actually managing to score. After the game a reporter asked Piniella why he ignored his third-base coach. "I don't use a third-base coach," was Piniella's facetious reply.

Diamonds Forever gathers together quotes from some of the larger-than-life characters associated with baseball as players, managers, owners, journalists and commentators. But because there is a whole literature and mystique surrounding baseball's past and present, a collection such as this can only scratch the surface. We have tried to cover the whole playing field, so to speak, with quotes about the beauty and uniqueness of the game as well as deep insights and flashes of wisdom. But as a humorist, the laugh-out-loud quotes about the quirkiness of the game and the people associated with it fascinate me the most. Enjoy!

W.P. Kinsella
White Rock, B.C., 1996

The
Mystery
of the
Game

In the beginning there was the word, and the word was "Play Ball."

George Bowering

Writer

How can you think and hit at the same time?

Yogi Berra

While a New York Yankees catcher

They give you a round bat and they throw you a round ball. And then they tell you to hit it square.

Willie Stargell

While a Pittsburg Pirates first baseman, 1978

What it adds up to is that it is not baseball's responsibility to fit itself into our frantic society. It is, rather, society's responsibility to make itself worthy of baseball.

That's why I can never understand why anybody leaves the game early to beat the traffic. The purpose of baseball is to keep you from caring if you beat traffic.

Bill Vaughan

While a *Kansas City Star* columnist, 1970

6

It happens in a thousand diamonds in so many different towns and villages. We pass them on the highway, these summer roadside attractions. Games played full of meaning for a few spectators and players and of no consequence to anyone else—never to be recorded. We reclaim them only in our memory and I suppose in our continuing fascination with this great game. It may not be life itself, but it sure feels like it.

William Humber

Canadian baseball historian, 1993

Correct thinkers think that "baseball trivia" is an oxymoron: nothing about baseball is trivial.

George F. Will

Political commentator, 1990

I think a baseball field must be the most
beautiful thing in the world. It's so honest
and precise. And we play on it. Every star
gets humbled. Every mediocre player has
a great moment.

Jim Lefebvre

Doctors tell me I have the body of a 30-year-old. I know I have the brain of a 15-year-old. If you've got both, you can play baseball.

Pete Rose

Baseball's all-time hit leader,
while a member of the Cincinnati Reds, 1985

It's the same as any other ball game
you'll remember as long as you live.

Joe Garagiola

Former player and broadcaster,
on playing in the World Series

Defense is baseball's visible poetry and its invisible virtue.

Thomas Boswell

Baseball writer, 1984

I broke in with four hits and the writers promptly decided they had seen the new Ty Cobb. It took me only a few days to correct that impression.

Casey Stengel

Former Major League player and manager

Fans, for the past two weeks you have been reading about the bad break I got. Yet today I consider myself the luckiest man on the face of the earth. I have been in ballparks for seventeen years, and have never received anything but kindness and encouragement from you fans. Look at these grand men. Which of you wouldn't consider it the highlight of his career just to associate with them for even one day? Sure I'm lucky. Who wouldn't consider it an honor to have known Jacob Ruppert. Also, the builder of baseball's greatest empire, Ed Barrow? To have spent six years with that wonderful little fellow, Miller Huggins? Then to have spent the next nine years with that outstanding leader, that smart student of psychology, the best manager in baseball today, Joe McCarthy? Sure I'm lucky. When the New York Giants, a team you would give your right arm to beat, and vice versa, sends you a gift—that's something. When everybody down to the groundskeepers and those boys in white coats remember you with trophies—that's something. When you have a wonderful mother-in-law who takes sides with you in squabbles with her own daughter—that's something. When you have a father and a mother who work all their lives so you can have an education and build your own body—it's a blessing. When you have a wife who has been a tower of strength and shown more courage than you dreamed existed—that's the finest I know. So I close in saying that I may have had a tough break, but I have an awful lot to live for.

Lou Gehrig

Farewell speech delivered by the future Hall of Famer at Yankee Stadium on July 4, 1939, often called "Baseball's Gettysburg Address"

I never knew how someone dying could say he was the luckiest man in the world. But now I understand.

Mickey Mantle

New York Yankees star outfielder,
on his own retirement and that of Lou Gehrig

What I am, what I have, what I am going to leave behind me—all this I owe to the game of baseball, without which I would have come out of St. Mary's Industrial School in Baltimore a tailor, and a pretty bad one, at that.

Babe Ruth

Baseball's greatest star, 1948.

All you have to do is pick up a baseball. It begs to you: throw me. If you took a year to design an object to hurl, you'd end up with that little spheroid: small enough to nestle in your fingers but big enough to have some heft, lighter than a rock but heavier than a hunk of wood. Its even, neat stitching, laced into the leather's slippery white surface, gives your fingers a purchase. A baseball was made to throw. It's almost irresistible.

Dave Dravecky

Former San Francisco Giants pitcher, 1990

It's fun, it's timeless, it's a relationship between a father and a son, it's a transition into manhood. It's a great zen game.

Bill Lee

Former Major League pitcher, 1994

It is designed to break your heart. The game begins in the spring, when everything else begins again, and it blossoms in the summer, filling the afternoons and evenings, and then as soon as the chill rains come, it stops and leaves you to face the fall alone. You count on it, you rely on it to buffer the passage of time, to keep the memory of sunshine and high skies alive, and then, just when the days are all twilight, when you need it most, it stops.

A. Bartlett Giamatti

Future commissioner of baseball, 1977

Almost the only place in life where a sacrifice is really appreciated.

Mark Beltaire

On the definition of baseball

The other sports are just sports.
Baseball is a love.

Bryant Gumbel

Broadcaster, 1981

Baseball, my son, is the cornerstone of civilization.

Dagwood Bumstead

As drawn by Chic Young

The whole history of baseball has the quality of mythology.

Bernard Malamud

Novelist

When I think of a stadium, it's like a temple. It's religious. Sometimes I go to Dodger Stadium just to be alone.

Jim Lefebvre

In the end all of our [baseball] authors leave us contemplating Roger Angell's witty aphorism. It seems, indeed, that baseball may well have . . . been fortuitously invented just to remind us of all other things in life. Things like our lost childhoods, and like our endlessly repeated emotional trips through the travails of our own private basepaths, in hopeless search for a misplaced route back home. It is a grand game, a thinking man's game, and a thinking woman's game as well. It is a game which surely does not mean half of the things we take it to mean. Then again, it probably means so much more.

Peter C. Bjarkman

Baseball historian, 1994

I believe in the Rip van Winkle theory—that a man from 1910 must be able to wake up after being asleep for seventy years, walk into a ballpark and understand baseball perfectly.

Bowie Kuhn

While baseball commissioner

The beauty and joy of baseball is not having to explain it.

Chuck Shriver

While a Chicago Cubs public relations official

I remember the last season I played. I went home after a ballgame one day, lay down on my bed, and tears came to my eyes. How can you explain that? It's like crying for your mother after she's gone. You cry because you love her. I cried, I guess, because I loved baseball and I knew I had to leave it.

Willie Mays

Hall of Fame outfielder

The Baseball Hall of Fame in Cooperstown, N.Y., sends a questionnaire to every ex-Major Leaguer it can find. One of the questions is "If you had to do it over, would you play professional baseball?" In all the years the questionnaire has been in existence no one has ever said No.

W.P. Kinsella

Novelist

It is the perfect cure for ulcers . . .

W.D. Valgardson

Writer

Y ou see, you spend a good piece of
your life gripping a baseball, and in the
end it turns out that it was the other
way around all the time.

Jim Bouton

Major League pitcher, 1970

Humor

The secret of managing is to keep the guys who hate you away from the guys who are undecided.

Casey Stengel

Former Major League player and manager

It's not big if you look at it from the standpoint of the national debt.

Bill Rigney

While manager of the Minnesota Twins, 1970,
on his club's ERA

Since 1946, the Cubs have had two problems: They put too few runs on the scoreboard and the other guys put too many. So what is the new management improving? The scoreboard.

George F. Will

Political commentator, 1982

As a nation we are dedicated to keeping physically fit—and parking as close to the stadium as possible.

Bill Vaughan

While a *Kansas City Star* columnist, 1981

When you play this game 20 years, go to bat 10,000 times, and get 3,000 hits, do you know what that means? You've gone 0 for 7,000.

Pete Rose

Baseball's all-time hit leader

I knew we were in for a long season when we lined up for the national anthem on opening day and one of my players said, "Every time I hear that song I have a bad game."

Jim Leyland

While manager of the Pittsburgh Pirates

Cool Papa Bell was so fast he could get out of bed, turn out the lights across the room and be back in bed under the covers before the lights went out.

Josh Gibson

Hall of Fame catcher

I**f** you can't stand the heat, stay out of The Chicken.

Ted Giannoulas

The man who dressed up as the San Diego Chicken, when asked if he was uncomfortable during a 1980 heat wave

42

It's not that I don't like baseball. There's not much to dislike. It's great for athletes who get winded playing croquet.

Ralph Moyed

While a columnist for the
Wilmington News-Journal, 1988

If I'm breaking them, they're dying in style.

John Mayberry

While a Kansas City Royals first baseman,
on his unusual number of broken bats

44

If Satch and I were pitching on the same team, we'd clinch the pennant by July 4 and go fishing until World Series time.

Dizzy Dean

Hall of Fame pitcher on Satchel Paige

Statistics are used by baseball fans in much the same way that a drunk leans against a street lamp; it's there more for support than enlightenment.

Vin Scully

Broadcaster

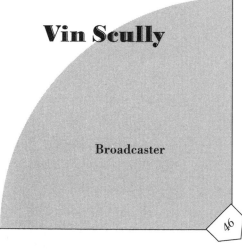

You know, I signed with the Milwaukee Braves for $3,000. That bothered my dad at the time, because he didn't have that kind of dough to pay out. But eventually he scraped it up.

Bob Uecker

Broadcaster and former player, 1984

It's easy to stay in the majors for 7 and a half years when you hit .300. But when you hit .216 like me, it's really an accomplishment.

Joe Lahoud

California Angels outfielder, 1975

In our day you could have gotten a live catcher and his family for $975.

Waite Hoyt

Hall of Fame pitcher, on being told in 1980 that
you could buy a bronze, limited-edition
sculpture of catcher Johnny Bench for $975

I believe there are certain things that cannot be bought: loyalty, friendship, health, love and an American League pennant.

Edward Bennett Williams

While owner of the Baltimore Orioles, 1979

A man once told me to walk with the Lord. I'd rather walk with the bases loaded.

Ken Singleton

While a member of the Baltimore Orioles, 1983

I told him I wasn't tired. He told me, "No, but the outfielders sure are."

Jim Kern

Texas Rangers relief pitcher recalling
when his manager took him out of a game, 1979

Your Holiness, I'm Joseph Medwick.
I, too, used to be a Cardinal.

Joe Medwick

Hall of Fame outfielder and former St. Louis
Cardinal, during a World War II visit
to the Vatican

One of my goals in life was to be surrounded by unpretentious, rich young men. Then I bought the Braves and I was surrounded by twenty-five of them.

Ted Turner

Atlanta Braves owner

54

If I ever find a pitcher who has heat, a good curve, and a slider, I might seriously consider marrying him—or at least proposing.

Sparky Anderson

While manager of the Detroit Tigers

The penalty is a little more than I expectorated.

Frenchy Bordagary

Major League outfielder
after being fined for spitting at an umpire

One day I was pitching against Washington and the catcher called for a fast ball. When it got to the plate, it was so slow that two pigeons were roosting on it. I decided to quit.

Paul "Dizzy" Trout

Former Major League pitcher,
on why he chose to retire

Putting lights in Wrigley Field is like putting aluminum siding on the Sistine Chapel.

Roger Simon

Columnist, 1988

One thing I do quite well is hit fly balls. There's nothing quite like being able to hit towering flies. It's not like writing Beethoven's Ninth, but it's definitely in the top two.

Charles Schultz

Cartoonist, 1985

Whenever an umpire settles down to reminisce about his career, he will invariably begin with the six most accurate words in the English language. It wasn't funny at the time.

Ron Luciano

Former Major League umpire

Baseball is a game where a curve is an optical illusion, a screwball can be a pitch or a person, stealing is legal and you can spit anywhere you like except in the umpire's eye or on the ball.

Jim Murray

Columnist

One of my chores was to milk the cows, which meant getting up before dawn and going out to that cold dark barn. I didn't expect to make it all the way to the big leagues; I just had to get way from them damn cows.

Edd Roush

Former Major League outfielder

I'll never forget September 6, 1950. I got a letter threatening me, Hank Bauer, Yogi Berra and Johnny Mize. It said if I showed up in uniform against the Red Sox, I'd be shot. I turned the letter over to the FBI, and told my manager Casey Stengel about it. You know what Casey did? He gave me a different uniform and gave mine to Billy Martin. Can you imagine that? Guess Casey thought it'd be better if Billy got shot.

Phil Rizzuto

Hall of Famer and
former New York Yankees shortstop, 1961

When I was a little boy, I wanted to be a baseball player and join the circus. With the Yankees I've accomplished both.

Graig Nettles

Former New York Yankees third baseman, 1979

Diamond Wisdom

A manager who cannot get along with a .400 hitter ought to have his head examined.

Joe McCarthy

Veteran Major League manager,
on managing Ted Williams, 1948

If they produce as well on the field as they do off the field we'll win the pennant.

Casey Stengel

While manager of the New York Mets,
commenting on his proposed outfield of Gus Bell,
Richie Ashburn and Frank Thomas,
who had 20 children among them, 1962

I have discovered, in twenty years of moving around a ball park, that the knowledge of the game is usually in inverse proportion to the price of the seats.

Bill Veeck

While owner of the Chicago White Sox

If you do everything right, you'll still lose forty percent of your games—but you'll also end up in the World Series.

Thomas Boswell

Baseball writer, 1989

Baseball is a kid's game that grownups only tend to screw up.

Bob Lemon

While manager of the New York Yankees, 1979

Kids are always chasing rainbows, but baseball is a world where you can catch them.

Johnny Vander Meer

While a Cincinnati Reds pitcher

That's the true harbinger of spring, not crocuses or swallows returning to Capistrano, but the sound of a bat on the ball.

Bill Veeck

While owner of the Chicago White Sox, 1976

A pitcher pitches low instead of high because how often have you seen a 420-foot ground ball?

Jim Bunning

Former Major League pitcher

They say you have to be good to be lucky,
but I think you have to be lucky to be good.

Rico Carty

Former Major League outfielder

If the human body recognized agony and frustration, people would never run marathons, have babies or play baseball.

Carlton Fisk

While a Boston Red Sox catcher, 1979

There are only two kids of managers.
Winning managers and ex-managers.

Gil Hodges

While manager of the New York Mets

A hot dog at the ball park is better than steak at the Ritz.

Humphrey Bogart

From a film ad for organized baseball

B aseball is dull only to dull minds.

Red Smith

Sportswriter

If you're not having fun in baseball, you miss the point of everything.

Chris Chambliss

While an Atlanta Braves first baseman

The two most important things in life are good friends and a strong bullpen.

Bob Lemon

While manager of the New York Yankees

Been in this game a hundred years, but I see new ways to lose 'em I never knew existed before.

Casey Stengel

While manager of the New York Mets

I am quite sure that statistics will show that the greatest number of successes have been scored by those who have led moderately dirty lives.

W.O. McGeehan

Sportswriter, on the habits of ballplayers, c. 1925

Any time you think you have the game conquered, the game will turn around and punch you right in the nose.

Mike Schmidt

Former Philadelphia Phillies third baseman

Pitching is really just an internal struggle between the pitcher and his stuff. If my curve ball is breaking and I'm throwing it where I want, then the batter is irrelevant.

Steve Stone

While a pitcher for the Baltimore Orioles

The longer I live, the longer I realize that batting is more a mental matter than it is physical. The ability to grasp the bat, swing at the proper time, take a proper stance, all these are elemental. Batting rather is a study in psychology, a sizing up of pitcher and catcher, and observing little details that are of immense importance. It's like the study of a crime, the work of a detective as he picks up clues.

Ty Cobb

Hall of Fame outfielder, 1950

They're like sleeping in a soft bed. Easy to get into and hard to get out of.

Johnny Bench

Hall of Fame catcher, on slumps

Fans don't boo nobodies.

Reggie Jackson

While a member of the Oakland A's, 1975

If a manager of mine ever said someone was indispensable, I'd fire him.

Charlie Finley

While owner of the Oakland A's

I remember the smell of fresh grass and the sun and the clean air. Now my boy comes down to the field and we have artificial turf and lights at night. You mostly smell stale hot dogs and phony grass, but the idea of baseball is still there. Baseball is an inheritance that's passed down from generation to generation.

Nelson Briles

While a Pittsburgh Pirates pitcher

. . . the only perfect pleasure we ever knew.

Clarence Darrow

Famous lawyer,
recalling baseball in his youth

Ninety feet between home plate and first base may be the closest man has ever come to perfection.

Red Smith

Sportswriter

Nothing flatters me more than to have it assumed that I could write prose—unless it be to have it assumed that I once pitched baseball with distinction.

Robert Frost

Poet

How to Keep Young

1. Avoid fried meats which angry up the blood.
2. If your stomach disputes you, lie down and pacify it with cool thoughts.
3. Keep the juices flowing by jangling around gently as you move.
4. Go very light on the vices, such as carrying on in society. The social ramble ain't restful.
5. Avoid running at all times.
6. Don't look back. Something might be gaining on you.

Satchel Paige

Hall of Fame Negro League pitcher, 1953

There is still nothing in life as constant and as changing at the same time as an afternoon at a ballpark.

Larry King

Broadcaster and columnist, 1990

Baseball is more like a novel than like a war. It is like an ongoing hundred-year work of art, peopled with thousands of characters, full of improbable events, anecdotes, folklore and numbers.

Luke Salisbury

Scratch an intellectual and you'll find a baseball fan.

Anonymous

Canada is a country whose main exports are hockey players and cold fronts. Our main imports are baseball players and acid rain.

Pierre Elliot Trudeau

While prime minister of Canada, 1982

The artist who says there is no beauty in straight lines has never seen a white sphere describing one just over second base.

Anonymous

I'm not the manager because I'm always right, but I'm always right because I'm the manager.

Gene Mauch

While manager of the Montreal Expos

Baseball is doomed. It is the inclusive
mesh of the TV image, in particular, that
spells . . . the doom of baseball now, but
it'll come back. Games go in cycle.

Marshall McLuhan

Social philosopher, 1969

What has happened is that all your life you operated businesses in such a way that you could one day afford to buy a baseball team. And then you buy the team and forget all the business practices that enabled you to buy it.

George Steinbrenner

While owner of the New York Yankees

Baseball is the only field of endeavor where a man can succeed three times out of ten and be considered a good performer.

Ted Williams

Hall of Fame outfielder

The pitcher has got only a ball. I've got a bat. So the percentage in weapons is in my favor and I let the fellow with the ball do the fretting.

Hank Aaron

Baseball's all-time home run king

$\mathbf{E}$very great batter works on the theory that the pitcher is more afraid of him than he is of the pitcher.

Ty Cobb

Hall of Fame outfielder

I wish I'd known early what I had to learn late.

Richie Ashburn

Hall of Fame outfielder

Potpourri

I once stood outside Fenway Park in Boston, a place where the ghosts never go away, and watched a vigorous man of middle years helping, with infinite care, a frail and elderly gentleman through the milling crowds to the entry gate. Through the tears that came unexpectedly to my eyes, I saw the old man strong and important forty years before, holding the hand of a confused and excited five-year-old, showing him the way. Baseball's best moments don't always happen on the field.

Alison Gordon

Canadian sportswriter, 1984

Thinking about things that happened, I don't know who could have done what he did. To be able to hit with everybody yelling at him. He had to block all that out, block out everything but this ball that is coming in at a hundred miles per hour and he's got a split second to make up his mind if it's in or out or up or down or coming at his head, a split second to swing. To do what he did has got to be the most tremendous thing I've ever seen in sports.

Harold "Pee Wee" Reese

Former Brooklyn Dodgers shortstop,
on Jackie Robinson, 1970

There's a couple of million dollars' worth of baseball talent on the loose ready for the big leagues, yet unsigned by any major league. There are pitchers who would win twenty games a season . . . and outfielders who could hit .350, infielders who could win recognition as stars, and there's at least one catcher who at this writing is probably superior to Bill Dickey, Josh Gibson. Only one thing is keeping them out of the big leagues, the pigmentation of their skin.

Shirley Povich

While a *Washington Post* sportswriter, 1941

I was thirteen years old and Jackie Robinson came to town to play an exhibition with the Dodgers. All the black folks in town turned out to see him. The old people, who could hardly walk, paraded down the main street with their heads high and the kids were dancing and a few people were being taken to the game in wheelchairs and even some blind people and the very sick. Nobody wanted to miss it. And I sat up there in the bleachers watching him and saying that would be me someday and when the train with the Dodgers pulled out, Jackie stood on the back platform like a political campaigner waving and smiling and making everybody feel good. I followed that train all the way down those tracks as far as I could run until the sound was gone and the tracks didn't rattle anymore.

Ed Charles

While a New York Yankees third baseman, on the day he decided to become a ballplayer

At the beginning of the World Series of 1947, I experienced a completely new emotion, when the National Anthem was played. This time, I thought, it is being played for me, as much as for anyone else. This is organized major league baseball, and I am standing here with all the others, and everything that takes place includes me.

Jackie Robinson

Hall of Famer and the man who broke baseball's color barrier

I was in Cooperstown the day Satchel Paige was inducted, and I stayed awake almost all that night thinking about it. It's something you never had any dream you'd see. Like men walking on the moon. I always wanted to go up there to Cooperstown. You felt like you had a reason, because it's the home of baseball, but you didn't have a special reason. We never thought we'd get in the Hall of Fame. We thought the way we were playing was the way it was going to continue. I never had any dream it would come. But that night I felt like I was part of it at last.

Buck Leonard

Negro League star and Hall of Famer

There is nothing greater for a human being than to get his body to react to all the things one does on a ball field. It's as good as sex; it's as good as music; it fills you up. Waste no tears for me. I didn't come along too early; I was right on time.

Buck O'Neil

Negro League star, 1981

As I think back now, the Negro Leagues served a great purpose by entertaining the downtrodden people who came to see them. At that time, we didn't have too many heroes. Remember this was before Joe Louis came along, and before Jesse Owens and Sugar Ray Robinson. I guess Jack Johnson and Harry Wills were the big heroes of that time. There weren't too many heroes to look up to, so these great baseball players filled this need.

Monte Irvin

Negro League star and New York Giants
outfielder, 1994

I never want to quit playing ball. They'll have to cut this uniform off me to get me out of it.

Roy Campanella

Hall of Fame catcher

As far as I'm concerned, there is no greater pleasure in the world than walking up to the plate with men on base and knowing that you are feared.

Ted Simmons

Former Major League catcher

The greatest player I ever saw was a black man. He's in the Hall of Fame, although not a lot of people have heard of him. His name is Martin Dihigo. I played with him in Santo Domingo in winter ball in 1943. He was the manager. He was the only guy I ever saw who could play all nine positions, run and was a switch hitter. I thought I was havin' a pretty good year myself down there and they were walkin' him to get to me.

Johnny Mize

Hall of Fame first baseman

If my uniform doesn't get dirty, I haven't done anything in the baseball game.

Rickey Henderson

While an Oakland A's outfielder

No, I don't have any regrets. Not about one damned thing. I've had a lot of good experiences in my life, and they far out-number the bad. Good memories are the greatest thing in the world, and I've got a lot of those. And one of the sweetest is of the kid standing out on the green grass in center field, with the winning runs on base, saying to himself, "Hit it to me. Hit it to me."

Pete Reiser

Former Major League outfielder

I've always been a firm believer that the game has never belonged to the owners. It has never belonged to the ballplayers. It belongs to that guy who puts his money up on the window and says, "How much does it cost to sit in the bleachers?" That is who owns baseball. And it has got to be kept that way.

Johnny Vander Meer

While a Cincinnati Reds pitcher

I have a theory: The larger the ball, the less the writing about the sport. There are superb books about golf, very good books about baseball, not many good books about football, and very few good books about basketball. There are no books about beachball.

George Plimpton

Sportswriter, 1982

You gotta be a man to play baseball for a living but you gotta have a lot of little boy in you.

Roy Campanella

Hall of Fame catcher, 1957

If you build it he will come.

W.P. Kinsella

Author of *Shoeless Joe*, 1982.
Spoken by Ed Harris as the disembodied voice
in the movie *Field of Dreams*

126

If I were playing third base and my mother were rounding third with the run that was going to beat us, I'd trip her. Oh, I'd pick her up and brush her off and say, "Sorry, Mom," but nobody beats me.

Leo Durocher

Long-time Major League player and manager

We're not football. We're not basketball. We're baseball and we're different . . . Why do we have to have a frenetic pace all the time? To people who don't know the game and can't appreciate the nuances, at times the game seems slow. Slowness and casualness *are* baseball.

Joe Brown

While an executive with the Pittsburgh Pirates

People ask me what I do in winter when there's no baseball. I'll tell you what I do. I stare out the window and wait for spring.

Rogers Hornsby

Hall of Fame second baseman

With those who don't give a damn about baseball, I can only sympathize. I do not resent them. I am even willing to concede that many of them are physically clean, good to their mothers and in favor of world peace. But while the game is on, I can't think of anything to say to them.

Art Hill

Sportswriter, 1980

Once upon a time in the midwest, they did something no one else has done. They were just kids, having fun and enjoying one another. They weren't thinking about being pioneers, about making history. They didn't realize what pioneers they were.

Lois Browne

Sports historian,
on the All-American Girls Baseball League, 1992

The play was unpredictable. Anything could happen, though usually routinely competent plays were made on routinely well-hit balls. You know the pace of good baseball: everything is going along in a comforting way, the reliable excellence almost lulling you to sleep, your attention beginning to waver a wee bit, when suddenly the opposition has runners on first and third, no one out, and their main woman at bat. Main woman, that was perfect.

This is still my idea of heaven.

Susan E. Johnson

As a fan of the All-American Girls
Baseball League, 1994

I ended up in the *Orange County Who's Who* for work in physical therapy. I'm just as proud of that as I am of my baseball. One thing about our league: it gave a lot of us the courage to go on to professional careers at a time when women didn't do things like that.

Dorothy Kamenshek

A member of the AAGBL's
Rockford Peaches, 1994

I'd rather play baseball than anything . . . You loved the game and it became a way of life . . . My years with the Peaches were the best years of my life.

Dorothy Ferguson Key

A member of the AAGBL's
Rockford Peaches, 1994

Next to religion, baseball has furnished
a greater impact on American family life
than any other institution.

Herbert Hoover

Former U.S. president

When I was a small boy in Kansas, a friend of mine and I went fishing and as we sat there in the warmth of the summer afternoon on a river bank, we talked about what we wanted to do when we grew up. I told him that I wanted to be a real major league baseball player, a genuine professional like Honus Wagner. My friend said the he'd like to be president of the United States. Neither of us got our wish.

Dwight D. Eisenhower

Former U.S. president

This is really more fun than being president. I really do love baseball and I wish we could do this out on the lawn every day. I wouldn't even complain if a stray ball came through the Oval Office window now and then.

Ronald Reagan

While U.S. president, on playing baseball with old-timers while celebrating National Baseball Month, 1983

Ain't no man can avoid being born average, but there ain't no man got to be common.

Satchel Paige

Hall of Fame Negro League pitcher

What's That Again?

I've seen the future and it's much like the present, only longer.

Dan Quisenberry

Former Major League pitcher

I'm just happy I got out of that blood-bath without actual physical abuse.

Al Leiter

While a Toronto Blue Jays pitcher, after allowing
five runs in one inning in Toronto's 15-14 victory
in Game Four of the 1993 World Series.

They say you can't do it, but sometimes it doesn't always work.

Casey Stengel

Former Major League player and manager

Little League baseball is a very good thing because it keeps the parents off the streets.

Yogi Berra

While a New York Yankees catcher

You can't worry if it's cold; you can't worry if it's hot; you only worry if you get sick. Because then if you don't get well, you die.

Joaquin Andujar

Former Major League pitcher

I don't know if this is what you're asking. But I feel closest to God, like after I'm rounding second base after I hit a double.

Anonymous

Eight-year-old boy,
quoted in *Psychology Today*, 1985

If you come to a fork in the road, take it.

Yogi Berra

Long-time New York Yankees catcher

The best thing about baseball is that you can do something about yesterday tomorrow.

Manny Trillo

While an infielder for the Philadelphia Phillies

I t's déjà vu all over again.

Yogi Berra

Long-time New York Yankees catcher

It's what you learn after you know it all that counts.

Earl Weaver

While manager of the Baltimore Orioles, 1968

NOTES

3. From *Baseball: a poem in the magic numer 9* (Toronto: Coach House Press, 1967). Reprinted by permission of the author.
5. Quoted in *The New York Times*, April 2, 1978.
6. From *The Kansas City Star*, quoted in *The Sporting News*, April 15, 1970. Reprinted with permission from *The Kansas City Star*.
7. From "Just Another Roadside Attraction," *Dugout*, October 1993. Reprinted with permission.
8. From his syndicated column, April 8, 1990. Copyright © 1990, *The Washington Post*. Reprinted with permission.
9. From Lowell Cohn, "The Temple of Baseball," in *The Temple of Baseball*. Copyright © 1985 by Richard Grossinger, North Atlantic Books, Berkeley, California. Used with permission.
10. Reprinted courtesy of *Sports Illustrated*, June 17, 1985. Copyright © 1985, Time Inc. All rights reserved
12. From *Why Time Begins on Opening Day* by Thomas Boswell. Copyright © 1984 by Thomas Boswell. Used by permission of Doubleday, a division of Bantam Doubleday Dell Publishing Group, Inc.
17. Quoted in *The Sporting News*, August 16, 1948. Used by permission.
18. Taken from *Comeback* by Dave Dravecky with Tim Stafford. Copyright © 1990 by Dave Dravecky. Used by permission of Zondervan Publishing House.
19. Quoted by John Lott in "Still Pitching from a Different Mound," *Dugout*, April 1995. Reprinted with permission.
20. From "The Green Fields of the Mind," *Yale Alumni Magazine*, November 1977. Reprinted with permission.
21. From *Webster's New World Dictionary of Quotable Definitions* by Eugene Brussell. Copyright © 1988. Reprinted with permission of Prentice Hall.
23. Copyright © by King Features Syndicate. World Rights Reserved. Reprinted with special permission of King Features Syndicate.
25. From Lowell Cohn, "The Temple of Baseball," in *The Temple of Baseball*. Copyright © 1985 by Richard Grossinger, North Atlantic Books, Berkeley, California. Used with permission.
26. From *Baseball and the Game of Ideas*. Copyright © Peter C. Bjarkman. Used by permission of Birch Brook Press, Delhi, New York.
31. Copyright © by W.D. Valgardson. Used by permission of the author.
32. From *Ball Four*. Copyright © 1970 by Jim Bouton. All rights reserved.
36. Quoted in *The Sporting News*, April 25, 1970. Used by permission.
37. From his syndicated column. Copyright © 1982, *The Washington Post*. Reprinted with permission.
38. From *The Kansas City Star*, 1981. Reprinted with permission from *The Kansas City Star*.
39. Reprinted from *It's Anybody's Ballgame* by Joe Garagiola © 1988. Used with permission of Contemporary Books Inc., Chicago.
42. Reprinted courtesy of *Sports Illustrated*, July 28, 1980. Copyright © 1980, Time Inc. All rights reserved.
43. Copyright © by Ralph Moyed, columnist for *The Wilmington News-Journal*, quoted in *USA Today*, February 19, 1988. Reprinted with permission.
47. Quoted in the *San Francisco Examiner*, March 29, 1984.
48. Quoted in *The Sporting News*, June 21, 1975. Used by permission.
49. Reprinted courtesy of *Sports Illustrated*, August 18, 1980. Copyright © 1980, Time Inc. All rights reserved.
50. Reprinted courtesy of *Sports Illustrated*, November 26, 1979. Copyright © 1979, Time Inc. All rights reserved.
52. Reprinted courtesy of *Sports Illustrated*, April 9, 1979. Copyright © 1979, Time Inc. All rights reserved.
56. Quoted in *Baseball Digest*, September 1986.
57. Quoted in *The Sporting News*, March 11, 1972. Used by permission.
59. Reprinted courtesy of *Sports Illustrated*, December 23, 1985. Copyright © 1985, Time Inc. All rights reserved.
60. From *Strike Two*, copyright © by Ron Luciano. Used by permission of the Bantam Doubleday Dell Publishing Group, Inc.

61. From *The Best of Jim Murray* by James Murray. Copyright © 1965 by James Murray. Used by permission of Doubleday, a division of Bantam Doubleday Dell Publishing Group, Inc.

63. Quoted by Barry Stainback in *Sport*, December 1961.

64. From *God's Country and Mine*. Copyright © 1954 by Jacques Barzun. Used by permission of Little, Brown & Co.

67. Quoted by Joe Williams in *The Sporting News*, 1948. Used by permission.

70. From *The Heart of the Order* by Thomas Boswell. Copyright by Thomas Boswell. Used by permission of Doubleday, a division of Bantam Doubleday Dell Publishing Group, Inc.

76. Reprinted courtesy of *Sports Illustrated*, July 30, 1979. Copyright © 1979, Time Inc. All rights reserved.

77. Quoted by Maury Allen in *The Incredible Mets*. Paperback Library, 1969.

84. Reprinted with permission of the National Baseball Hall of Fame and Museum, Inc.

86. Quoted in *The Sporting News*, June 28, 1950. Used by permission.

88. Quoted in *Baseball Illustrated*, 1975.

91. Quoted by Harold Seymour in *Baseball: The People's Game*. Oxford University Press, 1990. Reprinted with permission.

94. Quoted in *Collier's Magazine*, June 13, 1953.

95. From *USA Today*, June 25, 1990. Copyright © 1990, *USA Today*. Reprinted with permission.

96. From *The Answer is Baseball*. Copyright by Luke Salisbury. Reprinted with permission of Random House, Inc.

98. Reprinted courtesy of *Sports Illustrated*, July 26, 1982. Copyright © 1982, Time Inc. All rights reserved.

101. Quoted by Ira Berkow in *The New York Times*, February 20, 1983.

106. Quoted by Roger Angell in *Late Innings*. Ballantine, 1983. Reprinted with permission.

109. From *Foul Ball!* by Alison Gordon. Used by permission of McClelland & Stewart, Inc., Toronto, The Canadian Publishers.

110. From *The Boys of Summer*. Copyright © 1971, 1972 by Roger Kahn.. Reprinted by permission of HarperCollins Publishers, Inc.

111. Copyright © 1941, *The Washington Post*. Reprinted with permission.

113. Quoted by Maury Allen in *The Incredible Mets*. Paperback Library, 1969.

115. Quoted by Mickey Herskowitz and Steve Perkins in *Everything You Always Wanted to Know about Sports but Didn't Know Where to Ask*. New American Library, 1977.

116. Reprinted courtesy of *Sports Illustrated*, July 16, 1981. Copyright © 1981, Time Inc. All rights reserved.

117. Quoted by James A. Riley in the foreword to *The Biographical Encyclopedia of the Negro Baseball Leagues*. Carroll & Graf, 1994. Reprinted with permission.

118. From *It Takes Heart*. Copyright © 1959 by Mel Allen. Reprinted by permission of HarperCollins Publishers, Inc.

119. Quoted by Roger Angell in *Late Innings*. Ballantine, 1983. Reprinted with permission.

120. Reprinted with permission of the National Baseball Hall of Fame and Museum, Inc.

122. Reprinted with permission of the National Baseball Hall of Fame and Museum, Inc.

124. Reprinted courtesy of *Sports Illustrated*, May 10, 1982. Copyright © 1982 Time Inc. "They Said It" by George Plimpton. All rights reserved.

125. Quoted in the *New York Journal-American*, April 12, 1957.

130. Reprinted with the permission of Simon & Schuster from *I Don't Care if I Never Come Back* by Art Hill. Copyright © 1980 by Art Hill.

131. From *Girls of Summer*. HarperCollins, 1992. Reprinted with permission.

132. Copyright © 1994 by Susan E. Johnson. Excerpted from *When Women Played Hardball*, published by Seal Press (Seattle, Washington).

133. Excerpt from *Women at Play: The Story of Women in Baseball*. Copyright © 1993 by Barbara Gregorich, reprinted by permission of Harcourt Brace & Company.

134. Excerpt from *Women at Play: The Story of Women in Baseball*. Copyright © 1993 by Barbara Gregorich, reprinted by permission of Harcourt Brace & Company.

146. Reprinted with permission from *Psychology Today*. Copyright © 1985 (Sussex Publishers, Inc.).

148